To Eliza

Love Grandpa Irwin
Aug 2023

Let's Share!

Friendship: *Sharing and Taking Turns*

Authors
Betty Gouge, Ph.D.
J. Thomas Morse, M.A.
Deanna Tate, Ph.D.
John Eickmeyer

Research and Editing
Lyn Huntley, Ph.D.
Mary Thrash, M.A.
Teri Gathings, M.S.
Linda Stanislao, B.S.

Illustrations
Linda Bleck
Cathie Bleck
(character development)

Published by Family Skills, Inc., Dallas, Texas.
Distributed to Book Trade by
Kampmann & Company, Inc., New York, New York.

*Family Skills, Inc. wishes to acknowledge and express our sincere thanks
to the hundreds of children and parents who contributed to the research,
design, development and testing of KidSkills™ interpersonal skills series.*

Library of Congress Catalog Number 85-45002

ISBN:

0-934275-13-0

Published in the United States by Family Skills, Inc.

Manufactured in the United States of America

My name's little Doofer.
Hi! How do you do?
May I share my story
Of sharing with you?

I'm learning to share.
Sometimes it's no fun.
Sometimes it's the hardest thing
I've ever done.

It's hard to share things
Like my most favorite bear.
I hide him so no one
Will know that he's there!

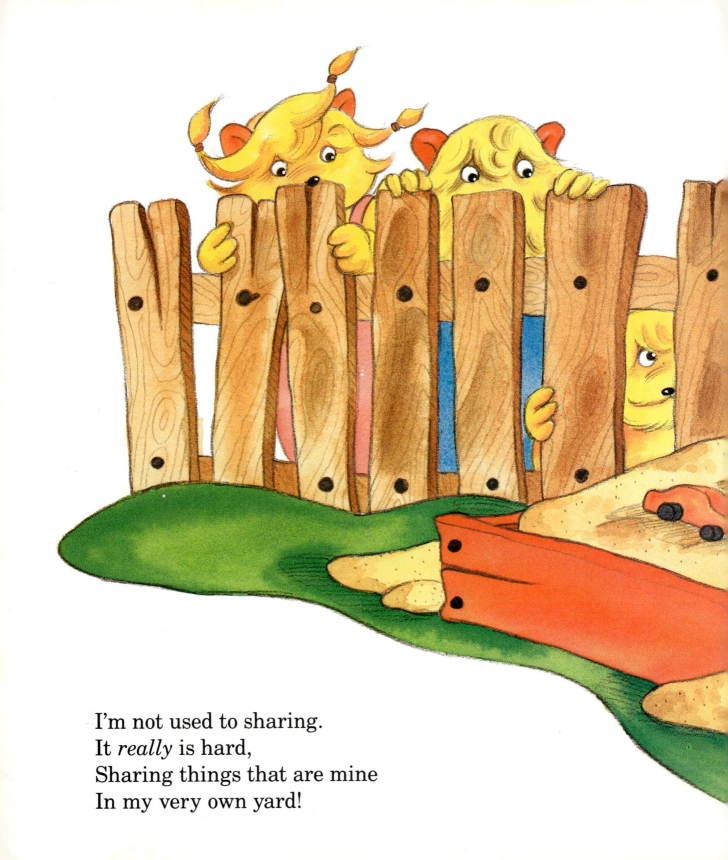

I'm not used to sharing.
It *really* is hard,
Sharing things that are mine
In my very own yard!

Sometimes I *must* share,
And then I feel mad
That I have to take turns
With the swing I just had.

I don't like taking turns
When I want something now.
Yet sharing means waiting
For my turn anyhow.

It's hard to say, "Please,
Will you share that with me?"
Sometimes I just grab
The first toy that I see.

I don't like hearing, "No!
You can't have this yet!"
When my friend has something
That I want to get.

But I'm *learning* to share,
So I'll share with you
Some things about sharing
That you can learn, too.

Before friends come over
To my house to play,
I pick out some toys
That I'll share that day.

The toys that I want
To keep all to myself,
I put in the closet
Or up on a shelf.

"I'm willing to share toys,"
I say to my friends.
We have fun when we share.
They say, "Let's play again!"

When I go to visit,
It's hard as can be
To get my friend
To share his toys with me.

I once took a trike
When my friend wasn't through.
He screamed and he cried,
And he stamped his feet, too!

So, politely I asked,
"When you're through, may I play
With your trike?" Then he smiled,
And he nodded, "OK!"

I'm learning to keep
My hands at each side.
I don't grab, and I ask,
"May I take a ride?"

When someone says "No!"
I don't like it a bit!
So I find a new toy
And I play with it.

When friends grab from me,
I say, "Please, leave that there!
Just wait till I'm through,
And then I will share."

My mom and my dad share,
So I watch what they do.
They share with each other
And share with me, too!

There's a family of ducks
That we feed everyday.
We have fun together
When we share and play.

Yes, I'm learning to share.
And I feel so proud, too
Because learning to share
Is a hard thing to do.

When you learn how to share,
I'll be proud of you.
You can share with your friends
And they'll share with you, too!

Keep sharing and sharing.
The more that you do,
You'll find that it's part
Of that wonderful YOU!

Other books from Family Skills:

Preschool:

Self-Esteem: *Adjusting to New Experiences*
Responsibility: *Making and Living With Choices*
Feelings: *Experiencing Feelings*
Responsibility: *Understanding and Accepting Limits*
Self-Awareness: *Accepting and Knowing Myself*

School Age:

Self-Esteem: *Being a Friend to Myself*
Cooperation: *Working Together*
Feelings: *Dealing With Feelings*
Listening: *Giving and Getting Attention*
Friendship: *Keeping Friends*
Friendship: *Making Friends*
Responsibility: *Making and Carrying Out a Plan*
Self-Talk: *Thinking and Feeling Good When Things Go Wrong*